Enjoying God

Enjoying God

Table of Contents

DEDICATION

For Kevin,
who first introduced me to
the concept of enjoying God

Rejoice in the Lord always.
I will say it again: Rejoice!

Philippians 4:4

Author's Note

This is a devotional book I have written for teens who desire to seek the heart of God and enjoy Him. If this describes you, I hope you will find these lessons helpful and encouraging. To get the most out of this devotional book, you will need a Bible and a notebook or journal.

When doing each lesson, I encourage you to take your time. You don't need to complete an entire lesson in one sitting. Do as much as you have time for, giving adequate thought and attention to each Bible verse or passage, question, and insights I share. Doing a small amount each day will be more beneficial than trying to do a whole lesson and rushing through it if your time is limited.

Another thing you may want to have on hand are some 3x5 index cards. Writing out verses you find especially meaningful and reviewing them several times a week will keep your thoughts focused on the truths you are learning.

With the love of Jesus,
Melanie

Think Differently

"Repent, for the kingdom of heaven is near."
Matthew 4:17

As you begin this devotional book entitled *Enjoying God*, I have a confession to make. I have not always enjoyed God like I should, and the concept is a relatively new one for me. I was raised learning about God, and by the age of thirty, I could have told you many things about God I had learned—some of them would have been right, some of them would have been wrong, but I would not have told you anything about enjoying Him. That isn't to say I wasn't, because I was to some extent, but I didn't classify it that way. I would have said, 'I'm living for Jesus,' or 'I am committed to serving Him,' but to say, 'I'm enjoying God, and I'm enjoying my relationship with Him.'—That wasn't a part of my vocabulary. I didn't think about it in those terms.

I believe God has been teaching me the importance of enjoying Him for the past several years. I don't know when it began exactly; I guess you could say Jesus enrolled me in *Enjoying God 101* without me realizing it until I was halfway through the course! At first He simply immersed me into an enjoyable way for me to go deeper with Him, and then once I came to grips with what was going on, I began to question if He was teaching me what I thought He was teaching me. Since then, through in-depth Bible study, listening closely to Jesus, and seeing the way God works in my life, I have become convinced of it.

Would you say you are currently enjoying God? Why or why not?

If you're like me, you may not have thought about the concept of enjoying God, and you're not even sure what I mean by that. If that's where you are, then this is the perfect study for you. Jesus and I want to take you there! So I hope you will come along on the journey with us. Start by reading the following verses in your Bible and write the words Jesus speaks in verse 17.

Matthew 4:12-17

Sometimes we get uncomfortable when we hear that word *repent*. It makes us feel guilty and like we can never get to where we should be in our relationship with God. But it's all in how you hear Jesus say it. If you hear Him saying it sternly with an accusing finger pointed your way, then yes, it's not a word anyone wants to hear. Even the most upright person could cower at that kind of image.

But I don't see Jesus saying it that way to me or anyone. I hear the love and compassion in His voice. The word *repent* means *to think differently*. Hear the words again, and this time imagine them being spoken in an urgent, pleading sort of way. Hear Jesus speaking them to you, not with harshness, but with gentleness and love.

> *"Repent. Think differently about Me. Get to know Me for who I really am. My kingdom is closer than you think, and it's a good place to be. So come close and let Me show you the way."*

How do I know Jesus meant it that way? How do I know the words were spoken with love? Because I know my Jesus, and that's the way He is. That's how He speaks to me, and I know He speaks to you in the same way.

In what ways do you think you may need to change your current thinking about God?

My purpose for this devotional book is not to lead you in my own ideas and ways of thinking, but to lead you in thinking rightly about our God. To lead you in the truth. It's a narrow path and few find it, but I hope you do. I hope you can learn to delight in your God. And it's not a false hope; it's a hope rooted in the truth that God loves you so much and He wants you to enjoy Him. He is pursuing you with His love, and if you believe that, it won't take long for you to be captured by it. But the key is: you must believe. You must think accurately about your God. You must be willing to say, like I did, 'Maybe I need to change my thinking.'

Read Matthew 4:17 again. Write the words of Jesus on an index card or somewhere you can review it often. What do you hear Jesus saying to you today?

Listen

"Hear, O Israel, the Lord our God..."
Mark 12:29

Good morning, good afternoon, or good evening. Whenever you have made time today to meet with God and listen to what He has to say to you, I'm glad you have. May you be richly blessed!

Read Mark 12:28-34

Who asked Jesus the question in verse 28?

What was his question?

What did Jesus say is the most important commandment?

I am in the daily habit of reading the words of Jesus. They are spirit and they are life, and the more I read them, the more I find that to be true. And they have become more to me than printed words on a page. They are the primary means by which God speaks to me. And I cannot tell you the number of times He has taken a familiar story or familiar words I think I completely understand, and He has done nothing short of turning it completely upside-down and saying, 'Un-huh. Read it again. Think differently. I have something new to teach you about that.'

What is the first word Jesus speaks in Mark 12:29 after the words, "The most important commandment is this:" (Or similar words, depending on the version you are using)?

Based on Jesus' words here, I believe that merely loving God is not the most important commandment. Loving God is a part of it, certainly, but it involves more than benevolent feelings and actions. Before Jesus says, 'Love the Lord your God,' He says, 'Hear.' *Before God wants us to love Him, He wants us to listen to Him. He wants us to understand who He is, that He loves us, and He is lovable.*

Would you agree with that? Why or why not?

How do you think listening to God and loving Him are related?

Here is another way I believe Jesus' words, and their counterpart in Deuteronomy 6:4-5 could be stated, based on Hebrew and Greek word definitions, and the complete context in which they are spoken.

> *"The most important commandment is this: Hear your God. Listen! He is Jehovah, the Eternal One. Don't listen to anyone else. Know Him for who He really is to the point you cannot do anything but love Him with your entire being."*

Read Genesis 2:15-17

In order to keep this command, Adam needed to first and foremost listen to God and believe Him. He didn't need to understand why the tree was bad. He didn't have to understand the command. He needed to understand *God* and believe He was trustworthy.

Read Revelation 2:7. Write the words of the first sentence.

These words are spoken by Jesus seven times. Once in each of the seven messages He had for the churches. And He could have just as well said, 'Hear God! Listen! I am your God."

From the beginning of the Bible to the end, the message is the same. He is our God and we need to listen to Him. He is worth listening to. He is worth trusting. He is worth loving.

How do you think knowing and listening to God could affect your enjoyment of Him?

Have you heard God saying anything specific to you recently? If so, what?

I don't know what He is specifically telling you, but whatever it is, I encourage you to listen. And hear Him say, "I love you." Because He does. Don't go by how you feel. Go by what He says. And believe it.

Joy In His Presence

"You will fill me with joy in your presence."
Psalm 16:11

One of the great things about truly following Jesus on a daily basis should be you simply enjoy being with Him. Take a moment to think about someone in your life you love to be with. What do you like about being with them? How do you feel when you are with them?

Do you feel you could "copy and paste" what you wrote about this person to fit this question: What do you like about being with God? How do you feel when you are with Him?

I could copy and paste:

I could **not** copy and paste:

Read Psalm 16. Look for things David enjoyed about God, and place them in one of two categories as follows:

I see God this way:

I need to work on seeing God this way:

Based on my own experience, I believe the most crucial element to enjoying God is to know Him for who He really is. To "see" what He is doing all around me. To recognize the security, direction, joy and eternal pleasures He brings.

For a long time I viewed God as Someone who asked far more from me than He gave. But the opposite is true. He gives far more than He ever asks, and one of the greatest things He gives is simply Himself. His constant presence to take joy in, not be threatened by.

Do you ever feel threatened by God? Explain.

What 'eternal pleasures' do you think David is referring to in verse 11?

What do the following verses say about 'eternal life'?

John 3:16

John 17:2

John 17:3

I think it's reasonable to assume eternal life as Jesus defines it is synonymous with the eternal pleasures David talks about. Eternal life isn't just about the future. It's about now too. It's about knowing and believing God. It's about enjoying Him. It's about enjoying His Presence and all the good things He brings.

What elements in your life do you consider to be eternal? (Hint: think about what brings you joy.)

Is there anything in your life you know should bring you joy but isn't? Why do you think that is? Talk to God about these things.

He Is and He Will

The LORD your God is with you...
Zephaniah 3:17

Before you begin today, review your answers in the previous lessons and any verses you have written on index cards. How is Jesus speaking to you so far? Have you seen evidence in your everyday life of God teaching you to enjoy Him, or through special circumstances? If you have, write them down in your journal. If you haven't, be aware of ways God may be revealing Himself to you in this area.

I received some news from a friend this week. My response to the news was, 'Wow, that's great. How exciting for you!' But her response was, 'No, it's not great. It's terrible. What am I going to do?' Why were our responses so different? Partially because she didn't give me all the details up front. But mostly it had to do with what we will be talking about today: The faithfulness of God.

My friend and I are coming from two different perspectives. My perspective is I've been through something similar in the past, and everything turned out great, even if there were bumps along the way. But my friend's perspective is mostly from all of the things that can be *potentially* bad about it. I emphasize that word, potentially, because most of her concerns and fears lie with things that *could* happen, not with what has *actually* happened.

The faithfulness of God is all about what actually happens. It's about the blessings God has for us. But blessings can often be disguised, especially in the beginning, as problems or trials.

What does James 1:2 say about trials?

What do verses 3 and 4 say about the purpose of trials?

Referring back to Psalm 16 we looked at yesterday, do you think David could know anything about the security of God if he had never felt insecure? Do you think he could appreciate the direction and guidance God gave him if he hadn't ever felt lost and directionless? Do you think he would be saying 'Keep me safe, O God, for in you I take refuge.' if he wasn't scared?

What are some situations you are currently facing that are making you feel insecure, scared, worried, or like you have no idea what to do?

Read Zephaniah 3:17. Write this verse on an index card. There are five promises stated in this verse. Write them out in first person. I'll get you started.

1. God is _____ me.

2. He will _____ me.

3.

4.

5.

He is, and He will. He has promised it! You might be on the front side of a bleak, confusing, scary, or hopeless path. Right now you can't see what will actually happen, all you can see is what could potentially happen, good or bad. And you have a choice. You can base your decisions, ways of thinking, and daily life on what you can't see. Or, you can base it on what you know about your God: He is faithful; He is with you and He loves you; you are delightful to Him and worth rejoicing over; and He is mighty to save.

Read Psalm 91. Write out anything you need to remember about who God is and the promises He has made.

Seeking and Seeing

"Seek first his kingdom..."
Matthew 6:33

If you have done my teen devotional *Heaven In My Heart*, the lessons for today and tomorrow will be familiar to you. I have included them in this devotional-study as well because they bear repeating and contain crucial elements of learning to enjoy God. As you review the Bible passages and the points I make, I pray they will fall fresh on you in regard to your current relationship with God and the current joys and trials you are facing.

In Matthew 6:33 Jesus tells us, *"Seek first his kingdom and his righteousness, and all these things will be given to you as well."* What this basically means is seeking God and the life He has for you is the most important thing you can do. It is life-changing. It matters. It is for your own good, not just something you should do because God or others say so. And no one can force you to do it. Seeking God is a choice for you to make for yourself.

Read Jeremiah 29:11-13

What does God say in verse 11?

What do you think it means to seek God with all of your heart?

When God says, 'I know the plans I have for you, and they are good plans!' Do you believe Him?

When He says, 'Pray to me and I will listen. Seek Me and you will find Me.' Do you believe Him?

There are many ways to seek God, and I believe some ways may work for one person that may not work for another. God wants you to enjoy Him, and in general, if you are getting to know God in an enjoyable way for you, then that's a good way for you. Don't force yourself to do things to seek God, learn about Him, worship Him, or serve Him in ways you don't really like. I am a shy and quiet person. My husband is loud and connects easily with anybody. We are very different, and we worship, serve, and learn about God in different ways. That's okay. You don't have to be like someone else. All God wants is for you to be yourself—after all, that is the way He made you!

But I would like to point out two ways that are very important if you want to seek God with all of your heart. One of them is reading the Bible. If you're doing this study, then you're on the right track there, and I will always try to point you to what God has to say about things, not just give my own opinion. Reading the Bible for yourself is important because it helps you to learn to listen *to God*, not just listen to what others say about Him. And listening to God is an important part of not just knowing *about* Him, but *knowing Him* by hearing what He has to say *to you*. He has plans for you that aren't like plans He has for anyone else, and only He can show you.

I would suggest you alternate days between doing this devotional book and reading the Bible on your own. Not with another Bible study, but just your Bible and your journal. Tomorrow's lesson will show you how to go about reading the Bible on your own. Pick a place in the Bible to start reading and do that for one or two days, and then come back to the next lesson in this devotional book, and so on.

Another way of seeking God is to be looking for Him in your everyday life. If you're having a good day, thank Him for all the good things and learn to recognize that those things come from Him and He wants to bless you. Get in the habit of seeing your life as a gift from Him and thank Him regularly for the ways He has blessed you.

And if you're having a bad day or going through a difficult time, learn to go to Him and ask for His help. He is there, and He has a purpose for whatever you're going through. Don't ignore your problems or try to handle them yourself. Go to Him and say, 'This is really hard, God, and I need help! Show me what to do; Give me strength; Help me to love that person even though they hurt me; Help me to see You in this and to learn whatever You're trying to teach me.'

Start right now. Write out a prayer to God, thanking Him for the good things and asking for His help with the bad. Be honest with Him about how you feel and what you need. He is there with you, and He is listening.

Jesus, thank you for...

Jesus, I really need help with...

Listening To God

"Listen carefully to Me, and eat what is good,
And delight yourself in abundance."
Isaiah 55:2 (NASB)

Today is all about you and God. God speaking, and you listening. As I mentioned in the previous lesson, I encourage you to begin reading a specific book in the Bible and read on your own for one or two days and then do the next lesson in this book, and so on. Today I have lined out a specific way of reading the Bible and getting the most out of it. You will need a notebook or journal to record your thoughts. If you don't already have one, it doesn't have to be anything fancy. An old spiral notebook you only used partially or blank pieces of paper stapled together is adequate. Or you may make copies of the Journaling Format on pages 150-151.

Copy the headings and questions on the following page directly into your journal, and use this same form each day you read. In the future you may want to modify it or eliminate it altogether as you find what works best for you. But use this guide for now to help focus your thoughts and prayers. Some of the questions may not apply to everything you read, so just answer the ones that do.

If you don't know where to read, some good books to start with are Genesis, Psalms, any of the four gospels (Matthew, Mark, Luke, or John), Galatians, Ephesians, Philippians, Colossians, or 1 John. You can read one or two verses at a time or a whole chapter and focus on what stands out to you most. Before you begin, take some time to pray and see if God is leading you to a specific place to start, and then follow this journaling format:

Date_____
Today I read_____

What does it say? (Write out the exact words of one or two verses, or briefly summarize what is going on.)

What does this mean in my own words? (Restate the verse or passage as if you are telling someone else.)

How can this specifically apply to my life?

What changes do I need to make because of what it says?

How can this be an encouragement to me?

What do I hear God saying to me?

What is my response to Him?

What Pleases God

"You are my Son, whom I love;
with you I am well pleased."
Mark 1:11

One of the most crucial elements to enjoying God is to change our thinking. Some of what you think about God and have been taught about Him is accurate, but some of it is not. And if you are not currently enjoying God, or not enjoying Him as much as you would like, wrong thinking is probably ninety-nine percent of the cause. Wrong thinking leads to misconceptions about God, others, and yourself. For example, if you do not fully believe God loves you, then you do not think about Him as being perfectly loving, and you do not think of yourself as being completely loved. Both are false, but that doesn't stop our wrongful thinking from affecting the choices we make and how we feel. We are loved, but we don't feel it. God is loving, but we don't accept it.

Today we are going to take a look at Jesus. The Bible plainly tells us God loved His Son and Jesus believed in His Father's love. Read the following verses and write the words that are spoken here or in your journal.

Mark 1:11

John 15:9

Before we go any further, it's important to think rightly about Jesus. Jesus was God, but He came to earth as a man. It can be hard to wrap our minds around this concept, but think of it this way: God had been watching mankind mess up for centuries. He had tried various ways of getting people's attention and revealing Himself to them, and a few got it, but very few. Abraham, Moses, David, Daniel, the Prophets—they knew God and followed Him, but God wanted *everyone* to know Him.

So what did He do? He sent Himself to show the way, but He didn't come in all His glory and splendor. He couldn't. No one could look upon God and live: not even Moses. (See Exodus 33:18-23) So, He took the form of an ordinary person we could survive having in our presence. In Philippians, Paul talks about this phenomenon.

Read Philippians 2:5-8

Jesus not only became a man, but He became a humble man. Not a king or a prince or a rich person, but a servant. He had no credentials as a human being. He had no power. No influence. No name to gain Him special favor. He was a commoner from a poor family. He wasn't even a prestigious Jew of the day. He wasn't a Pharisee. He became a Rabbi (teacher) when He was older, but He started out as a carpenter's son.

The only credentials Jesus had were those given to Him by His Father. Read Mark 1:11 again. What were they?

Jesus was a child of God, and God loved Him. That's it. Who does that remind you of?

Jesus, in His human form, was just like you and me—or perhaps less than that if you are of noble birth, rich, or an American Citizen. Most of us have rights and privileges Jesus didn't have. But, for our purposes in this lesson, let's think of Jesus as being just like us. Humble and ordinary. And yet we are God's children, and we are loved. And that pleases Him. We don't need any other credentials to be pleasing to God. We already have all that's required, and we didn't have to earn it. He just gave it to us!

Read 1 John 3:1. Write this verse on an index card.

Do you believe you are a child of God? Why or why not?

Do you believe God loves you fully and unconditionally? Why or why not?

What do you hear your Father (God) saying to you today?

Father, I trust you with...

A Display of His Glory

"Glory has come to me through them."
John 17:10

The Bible is all about how God connects with people and how people connect with God. As a novelist, I am very aware of most stories fitting into one of two categories: plot-based or character-based. As the names suggest, plot-based novels are mainly about the plot of the story: what happens, what obstacles need to be overcome, and the outcome. But character-based novels are more about the characters themselves. What they are doing and obstacles they are facing come into play, but it's more about how they respond to their situations and grow through them, not just survive. Readers will not only be concerned about the outcome of the story, but the people also. Some stories are heavily plot-based and some are heavily character-based, and others are a good mix of the two.

I see the Bible as being a mix of plot and character. It certainly has a good overall story and a great ending! But at the heart of it are the people involved in the plot. It's God's story, and He is the main character, but without the people, He wouldn't play the role He plays. Together with God, people are the story. And there are two main types of people: those who knew God and followed Him, and those who didn't. And similarly, those who experienced God's blessings and those who didn't: the two go hand in hand.

The Bible tells us we can and should learn from people of the past. And we can learn a lot about how we should live by reading about the various people in the Bible. You probably have your favorite characters and those you can relate to more than others. But as valuable as it is to learn from people like Moses and Paul and Ruth and Queen Esther, the person we have the most to learn from is Jesus. And while your current view of Jesus may be largely plot-based (He came, He died for our sins, He rose from the dead), the Gospels are filled with the character of Jesus. A lot of the time you have to read between the lines to catch His character, but it's there and it's vital to your understanding of Jesus and your journey with Him.

Read the following verses. What do they tell you about the character of Jesus?

John 5:17-19

John 8:28-29

Mark 5:22-34

Mark 5:39-43

In John 5 when Jesus called God His Father and claimed to be doing the same work He was doing, Jesus was making a serious statement about who He was. Not just a rabbi. Not just another teacher. He was making Himself equal with God. He wasn't merely following God, He was God. He was setting Himself up as their leader, and He had the miraculous power to prove it. And yet when He healed the woman in the crowd and raised the little girl back to life, He did so quietly. He didn't make their healing into public displays of His glory, He made it about them. He tells the woman her faith has healed her. He meets privately with the family of this little girl to raise her from the dead. In both cases, there were plenty of people around He could have "shown off" for, but He doesn't. His compassion moves Him, not the opportunity for glory.

What does Jesus say in John 17:10? Write this verse on an index card.

How do you think Jesus can receive glory through you?

I used to think I could only bring God glory with the things I did for Him. But it's not about what I can do for Him, it's about what He can do for me. He cares about my needs. He has compassion for the physical or emotional pain I'm experiencing. Letting Him heal me and bless me; living in obedience to Him *for my sake*; teaching others about the great things He has done *for me*: this is what brings Him glory.

In Philippians 3:14, Paul says, *"I press on toward the goal to win the prize for which God has called me heavenward."* Some people think this prize is some kind of crown or reward Paul would receive once he got to Heaven, but I don't think Paul was after anything except the same thing Jesus was in His obedience to death on a cross.

What was "set before" Jesus according to Hebrew 12:2?

What does Jesus promise to those who remain (abide) in Him? (John 15:7-11)

Spend some time praying right now about how you can be a display of His glory. It's about what God wants to do for you. It's about receiving His mercy. It's about the ways you need to follow Him to allow Him to bless you. It's about your relationship with Him. It's about how you can receive His love more fully and remain in it. It's about the joy He wants for you. Allow God to answer the following questions as you pray out loud or write one in your journal.

How can I be a display of Your glory?

What do You want to do for me?

What do I need to do to allow You to bless me?

What do I need to give up to allow You to bless me?

How can I receive Your love more fully?

How can my joy become more complete?

What do You want me to ask for right now?

Following Jesus

"Come, follow me..."
Mark 1:17

As we've discussed in the previous lessons, Jesus became one of us. He came to Earth as an ordinary person with no credentials other than His status as a child of God. But why did He do that? Why did He come? If your answer is He came to die for our sins, you're right, but He also came for another reason. He came to teach us. He came to teach us about His Father, and He also came to show us how to connect with God. That is our focus today and a crucial part of learning to enjoy Him. Jesus did it, and we can too.

Read Mark 1:9-20

What different things did Jesus do or encounter in these verses?

How many of those same things have you done or experienced, maybe not exactly the same way, but similarly?

What have you not done or experienced?

I was baptized when I was ten years old, and I believed God loved me and I was His child; I have been tempted many times to make the wrong choices and to turn away from God; I believe I've had angels looking out for me since I was born and they have protected me and provided for me when I needed that; I have taught the Good News and encouraged people to change their thinking about God; and I am living a life I would be comfortable with others following my example (most of the time, anyway).

I don't say that to be arrogant, I say it because that's what Jesus wants for me. He came to show us how to live. He wants us to believe we are loved children of God, because we are! He wants us to believe in Divine protection and provision, because it's real. He wants us to share the good news of God's love with others, because it's true. And He wants us to live lives others could follow, because we can be who God wants us to be!

Do you have trouble believing any of this? Explain.

In Mark 1:17-20, Jesus extends an invitation for some men to do what?

Jesus extends that same invitation to everyone today. Have you chosen to follow Him? If so, what does that mean to you?

I think one of the tragedies of modern Christianity is we see choosing to follow Jesus as a one-time event. When someone first hears about Jesus, or after they've been hearing about Him for awhile, they come to a decision where they decide to "follow Jesus". They walk forward in a church service, or say a prayer quietly in their heart; they know they are forgiven and believe they will have eternal life with Jesus; they may even begin to attend church regularly, change their lifestyle, and get involved in ministry, but something is lacking. It becomes something to be done on Sunday or a new way of life, but it's not really about following Jesus. It's about ritual or duty or feeling like they owe God something.

But following Jesus isn't about attending church or doing good deeds or being involved with other believers. Those things can and should be a part of following Jesus, but there's more to it than that.

What does Mark 1:18 say?

Jesus made God exciting! These men *wanted* to follow Him. They left their lives behind for it. Read a more detailed account of their calling to be disciples of Jesus in Luke 5:1-11. What did Jesus do to get their attention?

When Jesus performed this miracle right before their eyes and then called them to follow Him, in effect He was saying, 'You think that's cool? Just wait until I teach you how to do something even better and more important than catching fish!"

Look back at what following Jesus means to you. Do you feel like something might be missing in your experience of Him?

I shared earlier I believe God loves me and has angels protecting me and I have taught others about God and been following Him; but up until a few years ago, I did and believed those things on a limited scale: kind of the bare minimum of what I could believe and do and still call myself a Christian. I called myself a follower of Jesus, and I was following Him, but not in an abundant and exciting way like His earliest disciples seemed to do. I was following Jesus, but in many ways I wasn't enjoying it.

In a previous lesson you read about Jesus' status as a humble servant in Philippians 2. Read verses 12-13 today.

Back in verse five it says our attitude should be the same as Jesus' attitude. What was His attitude? He wasn't here to be God, He was here to follow God. He was here to show us how to connect with God and follow Him. "Follow Me!" He says to Peter and Andrew. 'Let Me show you how it's done! You can do this just the same as Me.' And they wanted to. They wanted to know God and experience His power.

Were they scared? I'm sure they were. They were probably shaking and trembling in their sandals, but they went. They followed Him because they knew He was worth following. They knew He had good places to lead them. They knew there was purpose in the madness! And considering the fact they remained with Jesus for three years up until His death, and then eagerly followed Him for years after His resurrection until their own deaths, I think they had a blast! I think they were scared out of their minds a lot of the time, but they enjoyed their God. Jesus taught them how, and they lived it, and "in fear and trembling" they were a part of changing the world.

According to His own words in John 15:9-11, why did Jesus follow God and teach others to do the same?

Do you think it's reasonable to assume if Jesus wanted His followers to have complete joy, He had it Himself?

In what ways are you experiencing joy in your life?

What things are a burden to you?

Talk to God about these things.

A Reason To Believe

He could not do any miracles there...
and he was amazed at their lack of faith.
Mark 6:5,6

The book of Mark reads like a whirlwind of all of Jesus' activity.   It doesn't begin with the genealogy of Jesus or His birth in a lowly stable. It begins with His public ministry when He was thirty years old, and it just keeps going until His death, resurrection, and going back to Heaven. And there aren't a lot of pit-stops along the way of the parables Jesus taught or bonding-times with His disciples. It's mostly one miracle after another until Mark gets to the week of Passover, and then he slows down a little and gives more details about that historic event.

Of the four Gospels, I find Mark to be the most difficult to glean more from the printed words than what's on the surface. But Mark is probably the easiest to read. It's a good book for someone who wants an overall view of Jesus' ministry years, but not for getting into the character of Jesus—unless you're in the mood to dig deep. We are going to be exploring such a passage today.

Read Mark 6:1-6.   Where did Jesus go at this time, and what happened there?

Why do you think the people had so little faith?

It's obvious from the text that many of Jesus' family members, friends, and the people who had watched Him grow up didn't believe who He claimed to be. To them He was just an ordinary man, and because of their lack of faith, Jesus wasn't able to prove otherwise. Imagine for a moment you have the gift of healing and you've been all over the world healing people and becoming famous for your miracles, and then you come back home and you can't heal a family member or close friend who needs it. How would that make you feel?

Why do you think God would have chosen this particular community for Jesus to be raised in if the people there were going to be among the faithless?

One of the keys to understanding what Jesus did and said is understanding the culture and religious system of the day. I'm not a scholar of Judaism or of the Jews living at this particular time, but one thing I have come to see simply by reading the Gospels is there was a huge gap between what Jesus was teaching and what the religious leaders of the day were teaching, and between how Jesus said to live and the way they were living. Jesus spoke harshly to them most of the time, and I think the commoners living then had to be confused about what they had been hearing in the synagogue for years and what Jesus said when He came. The Pharisees talked about ritual and piety (devotion and holiness), but Jesus' message was primarily one of love. He didn't even make His disciples wash their hands before they ate! How could He possibly be from God?

I believe the people fell into a trap that is similar to one we also fall into very easily. They didn't see Jesus as anything special because they didn't believe God wanted to do anything special for them. 'Why would God raise His Son in our humble town? Why would the Messiah be in my family? That doesn't make any sense. We're not nobility. We're poor, and Nazareth is a slum. Everyone in Israel knows that. How could anyone special come from here?'

Speaking from a purely human perspective of value and worth, is there anything about you that sets you apart from the average person? (Imagine a newspaper reporter drops by your house to do an interview with you for an article she's writing, and she says it's going to be on the front page of tomorrow's paper. Would you be able to tell her anything about yourself thousands of readers would bother reading?)

If you couldn't think of anything, don't feel bad. I'm sure Jesus wouldn't have much to claim either. 'Well, I am the Son of God— God Himself actually—but no one really believes that except my mother and my best friend. Other than that, I was born in a barn, raised in Nazareth—' (At this point the reporter breaks in with a laugh: 'Excuse me, did you say Nazareth? Oh, my, look at the time. I really must be going now.')

As I said earlier, the book of Mark can be difficult to study in-depth, but I read these verses the other day, and the text below is what God laid on my heart and I recorded in my journal.

When you know someone—or at least think you know them—you are not as quick to believe they could be anything special because they are just like you, and if you don't see yourself as anything special, it's pretty difficult to see them as such. But if you live with the belief that everyone is special to God and He can and will use you, then you will believe it when you see the spectacular in others.

Their lack of faith (& ours) may not be so much about a lack of faith in God, but a lack of understanding of how He works. And their lack of faith extends inward to a lack of faith in themselves and a lack of belief in their worth in God's eyes.

To do great things, we must believe we are great in God's eyes and He has great plans for us. If Jesus' family and friends would have believed they were special in God's eyes—chosen as the 'holy community' to know the Son of God personally, they would have believed Jesus was who He said He was and embraced Him wholeheartedly!

My prayer for myself is that I will always see myself as special in God's eyes. I believe this will go a long way to helping me reach the full potential of all He wants me to be. And it helps me to believe in the reality that I can be a vessel of the spectacular—because *He is spectacular and He lives in me!*

Who am I that I should believe such things? I am His child, and I am loved. And so are you!

Think about the needs and desires you have. Do you believe Jesus is able to meet those needs and fulfill those desires, even those that seem impossible?

If you do believe in God's ability to answer your prayers, do you also believe *you are special enough* for Him to do these things for you?

If so, do you also believe you are special enough to Him that He will sometimes say 'no' to things He knows are not in your best interests?

How you answer the above questions is all dependent on what you believe about God, how much you believe you are loved, and how much you believe in His desire to bless you.

What do you want to ask Him for today?

God Is Love

"For God so loved the world..."
John 3:16

Have you ever known someone who is the spitting image of their mother or father? They look like them, they talk like them, they have the same personality, sense of humor, or talents? Perhaps you are very much like one of your parents or a grandparent or an aunt. Many people say I look and act very much like my older sister. She is ten years older than me, and when I was young, a lot of my friends thought she was my mom because we looked so much alike, and then when I got older, people would ask if we were twins.

There are some verses in the Bible where it says, so to speak, that Jesus is the spitting image of His Father. (John 12:44-45) Jesus said they are one. (John 10:30) Now, we could get into a discussion about the Trinity here, but I'd like to divert our path in another direction. Today we are going to be looking at God's love for us and how Jesus is a part of that love.

Read John 1:17-18

What came through Jesus Christ?

Who made God known?

In 1 John 4:16 it says, *God is love.* And here we see love was revealed through Jesus Christ. Jesus is the image of His Father. He is love.

Read Mark 14:12-26

In case you are not familiar with the Jewish holiday known as Passover, let me give you a brief description of how it began and its purpose. If you go all the way back in the Old Testament and read about Moses and the Hebrew people while they were enslaved in Egypt, you will find the origin of Passover. God had cursed Egypt with many plagues, the final one being all of the firstborn males in each household would be killed. In order to protect the firstborn Hebrew males, God instructed His people to sacrifice a lamb and put the blood on the doorframe of their house. God said if they did this, their firstborn males would live because the LORD would *pass over* those homes.

God then told the Hebrew people to make Passover a yearly event—a celebration of God's deliverance—and He laid out a whole party-plan of how they were to celebrate. (You can read about it in Exodus 12 if you're interested in all the details.) And in Mark 14, this is what we see taking place hundreds of years later when Jesus was living in human form on Earth. Jesus was Jewish, or Hebrew, and His followers were also. So they took part in the annual festival, as their people had been doing for generations, to remember how God had delivered His people from death in Egypt.

What His followers didn't realize was they were about to have another kind of deliverance from death made possible by another kind of sacrifice. Jesus was the Lamb of God who was sent to deliver mankind from death for all time. Not physical death, but spiritual death. He had come to bring eternal life, and He was going to do it.

What does John 3:16 say about why God sent His Son? What was His motive? (*For God...*)

Read Isaiah 54:5-10 and John 13:1

I think sometimes we make the mistake of attributing love to the Father but not to Jesus, or vice-versa. We may look at the Father as sending His Son to rescue us from death because He loved us, and Jesus had no choice in the matter. Or, we look at the Father as having all of this anger and wrath toward us, and Jesus stepping in to fill the gap and make amends. But God's love is not compartmentalized like that. God is love. That is who He is. Not part of who He is, or who He is sometimes, but all the time in every way. Jesus was not sent to be a vessel of God's love, or make up for God's lack of love. He was God. He came to show us His love.

And that was the purpose of the Passover, to remind people of God's mercy and love, but for many I think it had become a yearly holiday where they went through the motions but didn't really take the meaning of it into their hearts. They were doing something because it was tradition, not because they grasped the meaning behind it. Yes, they may have been reminded of God's deliverance of their ancestors in Egypt, but I believe they had lost the message of it: *For God so loved the Hebrew people living in Egypt He made a way for them to escape death and flee the land of slavery.*

What does Jesus say in Mark 14:18?

In what way does this show at least one of the disciples didn't believe in the true meaning behind Passover?

I believe Jesus was saying, 'You don't get it! None of you! *One* of you is going to betray me, but *all of you* doubt God's love to some degree. You don't believe in God's deliverance. Something that happened hundreds of years ago has little meaning for you now. It's too abstract. You celebrate this every year, but you've forgotten what you're celebrating: My love for you. God's love for you!'

Jesus didn't have to shed His own blood to provide a way for salvation. Up until then, God had already been atoning sin for generations. From the beginning, He was merciful. But the people had lost sight of that. They needed a fresh reminder, a more convincing display of God's mercy. He Himself would die for them because He loved them so much. So He died. He became the sacrificial lamb. 'I'll die for you Myself, once and for all. No more sacrifices are needed. No more yearly celebrations. No more doubt. Just believe.'

God's love for us is the key. Not ancient covenants. Not annual celebrations. Not Jesus' death and resurrection. These things are *evidence* of God's love for us. But too often we focus more on the means by which God has saved us than His motive for doing so. We may believe Jesus died for us and rose from the grave. We may believe we are forgiven and will have eternal life. And yet somehow we continue to doubt God's love for us. We forget the message behind the historical events. We forget the most important element of Christianity there is: God is love.

Read 1 John 4:7-19. Write at least one verse from this passage on an index card.

In the following verses, what are we to do with God's love?

7-8:

9-10:

16:

17-18:

There is too much here and too much the Bible has to say about God's love for us to get into it all today. This is just the beginning of what I hope will be a fresh journey for you in your walk with Jesus and in your life as His beloved child. We'll look at more in the next lesson about the difference God's love for us can make in our lives, but for today I'd like to leave you with this interpretation of these verses by Eugene Peterson, the writer of *The Message*. Let them sink deep into your heart.

> *My beloved friends, let us continue to love each other since love comes from God. Everyone who loves is born of God and experiences a relationship with God. The person who refuses to love doesn't know the first thing about God, because God is love—so you can't know him if you don't love. This is how God showed his love for us: God sent his only Son into the world so we might live through him. This is the kind of love we are talking about—not that we once upon a time loved God, but that he loved us and sent his Son as a sacrifice to clear away our sins and the damage they've done to our relationship with God.*

Everyone who confesses that Jesus is God's Son participates continuously in an intimate relationship with God. We know it so well, we've embraced it heart and soul, this love that comes from God.

God is love. When we take up permanent residence in this life of love, we live in God, and God lives in us...There is no room in love for fear. Well-formed love banishes fear. A fearful life is one not yet fully formed in love. We, though, are going to love—love and be loved. First we were loved, now we love. He loved us first.

What does God's love mean to you today?

Love Is...

"I am the way and the truth and the life.
No one comes to the Father except through me."
John 14:6

When I was a young girl, I had a poster in my room of Mickey and Minnie Mouse. In the colorful drawing they were standing side-by-side, and Minnie was looking at Mickey with hearts coming out of her head, and on the top of the poster it said: LOVE IS...

I didn't get it. Often I would look at the poster and ask, 'Love is what?' I was a little young to understand Minnie was in love with Mickey, and it wasn't until I was older that I understood the picture itself gave the definition of romantic love: Being together; Looking at each other in that special way; Mickey giving Minnie a bright flower as a gift.

Even though there is more to love than the poster depicted, it actually was a good way of defining love. The picture told the story because love is something that is *displayed* in the way we act. You can't say you love someone and then do absolutely nothing to show that love.

God has showed us His love in many ways. He made us. He made a beautiful world for us to live in. He surrounds us with family and friends who care about us. He delivered our spiritual ancestors from slavery in Egypt and led them to the Promised Land. He keeps the world spinning and the sun coming up every morning. He died for us and rose from the grave. He forgives us and promises us eternal life. He hears us when we pray and comes to our rescue, even if we have run away and lived in disobedience. He has given us His Word and instructions for successful daily living. He promises to always meet our needs, and He does it! He blesses us in so many ways every day.

He is love, and He demonstrates that love. If we drew a depiction of any of the ways He shows us His love, we could put this caption at the top: LOVE IS...

Because the Bible says God is love and Jesus is the greatest demonstration of that love, I'd like to give you a little exercise today to help you grasp how vital that love is to our lives. We often talk about God's love, but living in that love is another matter. In fact, we often totally lay it aside without realizing we are doing so.

Look up the following verses and substitute the words "I am" with the words "Love is", and the word "me" or "I" with the words "My love". I'll get you started:

John 6:48

  Love is the bread of life.

John 8:12

John 10:7

John 10:11

John 11:25

John 14:6

John 15:5

Which of these speaks to you most today? Write your modified form of the verse on an index card.

God's love sustains us. We need it daily. His love is the light we need to find our way in the darkness. His love is the gateway to a right relationship with Him. His love guides us and protects us. His love raises us out of the grave and gives us new life. In His love we find the way, the truth, and the life He has for us. If we do not believe in His love for us, we cannot connect with Him on a personal level. His love is vital to our being. Without being connected to it and drawing our energy from it, we cannot live.

Personalize these word pictures for yourself. Complete the following sentences based on your needs, desires, and circumstances.

I need to remember God's love for me daily so I can...

I need God's love for me to light my path as I...

I need to base my relationship with God on His love for me instead of on...

God loves me and will always guide me, provide for me, and protect me, so I don't need to worry about...

I am living as a dead person in the area(s) of...

Jesus, help me to believe in your life-giving love so I can...

I am connected to God's love for me as I...

In order to be more connected to God's love, I must...

Write out these words at least five times.

God loves me.

Sprinkled or Immersed?

"...baptizing them in the name of the Father
and of the Son and of the Holy Spirit."
Matthew 28:19

What comes to mind when you think of the word "baptism"?

If you have been baptized, were you sprinkled or immersed?

The church has been arguing for centuries about the proper way, and if you're starting to feel uncomfortable I might say you weren't baptized in the right way or at the right age, don't worry, I'm not. This lesson is not about the proper way to be baptized in a physical sense. I don't think God cares, and I know I don't.

The Bible and the Judeo-Christian Faith is full of symbolism. God often used physical objects, practices, journeys, and stories to relate what is unseen to things that can be seen. For example: The vastness and diversity of Creation displays the reality of a really big God with big ideas; The slavery of the Israelites in Egypt represents how we can be enslaved to sin, and their Exodus to the Promised Land is a picture of God's desire for us to be set free to an abundant life.

Jesus called Himself the Bread of Life, the Good Shepherd, and the Living Water. That doesn't mean Jesus is a piece of food or a sheepherder by profession. He was describing Himself in ways people could relate to: He would meet their needs and sustain them; He would care for them; He satisfies a thirsty soul.

And the same is true of baptism. It's not about the water. It's not about how, when, or where. It's about the meaning behind it. What is God trying to show us through the practice of baptism? What does He want us to understand about our salvation when He commands such a ritual?

That is what we will be looking at today. So, sprinkled or immersed or not yet dunked—all are welcome. Let's look at the glorious realities behind this ancient and modern practice of baptism.

Read Matthew 3:1-6

Who was John baptizing?

What was his message? (verses 2-3)

What did the people do before they were baptized?

In addition to people today arguing about whether baptism should be done by sprinkling or full immersion in water, some also are convinced that because John baptized people in a river, that's the only acceptable place to be baptized today. But the choice of the Jordan River was a symbolic one, not because river water is somehow more holy than any other. The Jordan was a natural barrier between the desert and the Promised Land. Anytime someone entered into the Jordan River to cross over to the other side, they were entering a new land full of promise.

What was the promise the people who were baptized were counting on when they confessed their sins?

One of the symbolic principles behind baptism is the reality that we are forgiven. Just as water can make our bodies clean, God can make our hearts clean. This is the first thing to believe if you are thinking of being baptized or if you have been in the past—no matter when or where or how. You are forgiven. Not by the water, but the Living Water. Jesus alone brings salvation, and He brings it to all.

Do you believe God has forgiven you for your sins?

In addition to baptism being a symbol of "the washing of sin", it is also talked about as being symbolic of Jesus' death and resurrection. When we are put under the water, that symbolizes death, and being brought out of the water represents "new life".

Do you believe you are living a new life in Christ? How so? (If you have always known Jesus, think about how your life might be different if you didn't know Him.)

Read Matthew 3:13-17

What reason did Jesus give for wanting to be baptized?

Jesus never sinned. He did not need to be forgiven, so what other reasons do you suppose Jesus had for being baptized?

I believe there are many correct answers to that question, and until we have the chance to ask Jesus face-to-face (if we will even care at that point) we will never know all the reasons. But I'd like to share some of my own thoughts with you based on what takes place here and what I have seen take place in my own life. I was baptized by immersion in a Baptist church when I was ten years old, and it was a very real experience for me that meant something to me at the time. I believed in God's forgiveness, and I wanted to show others my decision to follow Christ. And for me at that time, that was enough. I had a very childlike faith, and I will never forget that day.

But as I grew older, I began to lose some of that faith. Not in 'go my own way' rebellion, but I did let go of God's love for me, at least partially. I never stopped believing God loved me in an intellectual sense. I never would have told someone, 'God doesn't love me', and I never had that conscious thought.

But some of my thinking about God became warped, and I began to think of God's love as being something I had to earn. And I also began to live my life and make some decisions and choices that did not reflect a belief in God's love for me. I began to feel guilty I wasn't "doing enough for God". Not because I wasn't doing anything, but because there's always more to do. And the way I thought about money, God's commands, and my personal well-being was based on my own logical reasoning rather than God's promises to always meet my needs, care for me, and lead me in the right way.

I needed a new kind of baptism. Not a physical one. Not to be "washed clean" again. But a baptism into His love. The word *baptism* does mean to be "immersed", but it wasn't a good dunking in a river I needed, it was a good dunking into His love!

I believe that's one thing Jesus was doing when He went down to the river to be baptized by John. He's not going to be made clean. He may have gone to be an example to others, or to symbolize His future death and resurrection, or to receive the Holy Spirit. But I think mostly He was going to remind Himself, 'My Father loves Me. I can be immersed in His love. I am His beloved child, and that's enough to please Him. I don't have to add anything else.' And His Father gave Him what He was looking for.

Have you been fully immersed in God's love for you, or only sprinkled? Explain.

Read Matthew 28:16-20

It is entirely possible to have been "sprinkled" as a baby and still experience the complete love of God. And it is also possible to be "immersed" as a child or adult and yet have very little experience with the reality of God's love in your life. To be "baptized in the name of the Father, Son, and Spirit" (Matthew 28:19) means you are completely immersed in all that He is. And He is Love.

I encourage you to pray about this now and in the coming days. Talk to God about His love for you and if you are experiencing it fully. Ask Him to show you ways you aren't and how you can change that. Don't let baptism be a one-time act. Be baptized every day into His unconditional and marvelous love, and *that* will change your life.

What do you hear Jesus saying to you today?

Living Water

*If you only knew the gift God has for you and who I am, you
would ask me, and I would give you living water.*
John 4:10 (NLT)

Begin today by reviewing the verses you have written on index
cards and choose one to memorize this week. Why does this verse
speak to you specifically today?

The Bible scene we are going to read for this lesson is one of my
favorites. It's not really a spectacular story. No great miracle takes
place. There are only two people involved. And the setting is
simple: a well of water people came to every day to satisfy a basic
need. The woman in this story who comes to the well is doing the
same, and yet she has a unique encounter with Jesus. A life-
changing encounter.

Read John 4:1-26

What is the first thing Jesus says to the woman, and how does she
respond?

What does Jesus say to her in verse 10?

Do you think of Jesus as someone who only wants things from you, or as someone who has much to give you?

When was the last time Jesus asked you for something? What was it? Did you give it to Him?

When was the last time you received something from Jesus? What was it?

Jesus does ask us for things at times. He may ask us to have more faith in Him and to trust Him. He may ask us to get involved in a ministry and help others in need. He may ask us to spend more time with Him and to study His Word. But He also wants us to ask things of Him. He wants us to ask for more faith. He wants us to ask for a desire to serve Him and direction in how we can best help others. He wants us to ask Him to meet with us and teach us. He wants us to ask Him for His presence in our lives.

Jesus does not need anything from us. He did not need this woman to give Him a drink. He could have gotten one for Himself. But He used this opportunity to make a connection with her. He asked her for something to start up a conversation, not just because He was thirsty and too lazy to get it Himself.

We need to think of Jesus' requests this way also. He's not in need of us to do His work. He can provide in supernatural ways for others just as easily as asking for our help. In fact, involving us probably takes more effort than for Him to do something Himself! He is fully capable of doing anything that needs doing.

So why does He involve us? Because He's looking to connect with us. Look back at what Jesus has asked of you. If you gave Him what He asked for, what was your motive for doing so?

Have you allowed it to be an opportunity to deepen your relationship with Him?

If you didn't do what He asked, are you feeling guilty about it? Is it hindering your relationship with Him currently?

When I lack the faith to do something Jesus is asking me to do, I have learned it's okay for me to say no. He does not condemn or punish me for that choice, but He does use it as a way of pointing out things in my mind and heart that need tweaking. It exposes my imperfection. It brings to light the needs of my heart I am not allowing Jesus to heal. It reminds me I'm a work-in-progress, and that's okay. Jesus does not want me to do things I'm not ready to do. He just wants me to be honest about why I'm not ready and then allow Him to help me in those things.

It takes time. It takes prayer. It takes a renewing of my heart. It takes a deeper understanding of God. It takes me believing in His goodness and the depths of His love for me.

It takes Living Water, and Jesus is the source.

What do you hear Jesus saying to you today?

The Empty Places

"Whoever drinks the water I give will never thirst."
John 4:14

If you enjoyed reading about the woman at the well, I have good news for you. We're not done with her yet. I'm going to have you read the story again, and as you read, try to look for things you didn't notice the first time. Remind yourself of what we talked about concerning what Jesus has to offer us. Imagine you are this woman. How would the words of Jesus make you feel?

Read John 4:1-29 and record your thoughts.

What do you think Jesus means when He says those who drink the Living Water will never thirst?

Given what you know about Jesus, what do you think are the elements of this Living Water?

In John 6:63, Jesus says, *"The words I have spoken to you are spirit and they are life."* I think Jesus is talking about the same thing here. When we listen to His words of truth, when we take in the love of God that Jesus came to show us, when we truly believe and live by His words, we experience a supernatural transformation. We feel satisfied. We become filled with love and joy and peace. We know we are loved, and that supersedes everything else. Our circumstances may be difficult, but we're content to let God take care of us. We wait with hopeful expectancy to see what He is doing and what's waiting for us on the other side of the valley.

Thirst can take many forms. There are emotional thirsts of dissatisfaction, loneliness, and heartbreak. There are spiritual thirsts of needing more of God's love and truth and an indwelling of His Spirit. Jesus says that those who *"hunger and thirst for righteousness will be filled."* (Matthew 5:6) Thirst can be a good thing because it makes us aware of our needs. And Jesus wanted to do this for the woman at the well. He wanted to expose her need and the empty places in her heart. That will be our focus for the remainder of this lesson.

What does the woman say to Jesus in verse 15?

How does Jesus respond?

What does the woman say to Him in verse 17?

Did Jesus already know that?

When this woman asks Jesus for the Living Water, why does He ask her to go get her husband? He knew she didn't have one, and His words seem out of place. A more appropriate response may have been, 'Have you been baptized? Would you like to be?' Or, He could have gotten into a discussion with her about Who He was and why He came. He could have said, 'Follow me. Come and be My disciple.'

But He didn't do either, and this is why: He wanted her to be honest about her emptiness. That was the key to receiving the Living Water because its purpose was to fill up those empty places in her heart. And it's the same for us today. Before we drink the Living Water we must first realize how thirsty we are.

Imagine you are meeting Jesus by this well. You ask Him for the Living Water, and He says, "Go and get your _____." What could He say where your only response could be, "I have no_____." (Think in terms of people, personal character, possessions, etc. Anything that you feel is missing. You can fill in the blank with more than one answer.)

You may have answered in terms of the people in your life. 'I have no close friends, no boyfriend, no time with my family, no role models.' Or in terms of personal character: 'I have no values, no self-respect, no hope of cleaning up my life.'

Or your words might be something more like, 'I have no patience with others. I have no strength to make it through the day. I have no way of controlling my anger. I have no goals. I have no talent. I have no peace. I have no...'

The list of our emptiness can go on and on. And it's entirely possible to have known Jesus for years without allowing Him to fill up those empty places. Receiving the Living Water requires your honesty about your losses, your weaknesses, your disappointments, your mistakes, and your deepest needs. But in exchange for your honesty, you will receive the love, the peace, and the blessings Jesus has waiting for you. He won't send you away empty-handed. He will fill you to overflowing. To really living. To life eternal.

What do you want to ask Jesus for today?

The Condition of the Heart

"No good tree bears bad fruit..."
Luke 6:43

I would like to begin today by asking how your independent Bible-reading is going. If reading the Bible on your own has become a regular habit for you, I hope you are finding it to be valuable. If it isn't something you do on a regular basis, or you find it frustrating, I encourage you to keep trying. You can refer back to "Listening To God" in the Table of Contents or visit the "Journaling Guide" as a reminder of what to look for as you read.

Today we are going to be talking about the specific topic of enjoying God, and if you feel I haven't been doing that much so far in this devotional book, it's true I haven't talked about it a lot in those specific terms. But everything we do to seek God, from reading the Bible, learning more about Jesus, and receiving His love, to going to Him with our concerns, emptiness, pain, and needs are a part of enjoying Him. As we will see today, enjoyment is not always happy or joyful. Sometimes it is disguised and takes other forms that are equally valuable to our enjoyment of Him.

In simple terms, to enjoy something is to experience something with joy. And when we think of enjoyment, we usually think of experiencing the emotion of joy. But it can also be an experience of pleasure, benefit, or satisfaction. At times these words may be synonymous with being joyful, but not always. Enjoying something or someone may not always mean your primary emotion is joy.

Similarly, joy does not always mean happy. Happiness is often a part of joy. But it can also manifest itself in other ways. Today we are going to be looking at the different forms "Enjoying God" may take. You may be enjoying Him more or less than you think.

Read John 15:1-11. List words in this passage that are repeated several times.

Read Galatians 5:22-26

List the characteristics of the "Fruit of the Spirit".

When we live by the Spirit, what character flaws should not be a part of our heart? (verse 26)

Do you struggle with any of these?

One way of defining the enjoyment of God is to say when we enjoy Him, our hearts are filled with good things. We love, we have peace, we have joy, we are patient with others and have patience about God's timing. Kindness, goodness, faithfulness, gentleness, self-control—we are characterized by these things.

Which of the elements of the Fruit of the Spirit do you feel you possess in abundant measure?

We can also measure our enjoyment of God by what's not there. If we are conceited and prideful, angry with others, or filled with envy, these are signs we are not enjoying God. In Luke 6:43-45, Jesus says, *"No good tree bears bad fruit, nor does a bad tree bear good fruit. Each tree is recognized by its own fruit...The good man brings good things out of the good stored up in his heart, and the evil man brings evil things out of the evil stored up in his heart. For out of the overflow of his heart, his mouth speaks."*

According to John 15:4-5, what is the secret to bearing good fruit?

What is the result of remaining in Christ and bearing good fruit? (verse 11)

At times, joy may take the form of happiness. But it might not. It might take the form of being beneficial: something that is to our advantage, even if it's a painful or challenging experience.

Can you think of something that has been beneficial to you, even though it also brought difficulty, pain, or sorrow?

Joy may also take the form of something that is satisfying. It may not be an especially pleasurable experience, but it may result in a feeling of purpose, accomplishment, or completeness. Ministry can often be this way. It may require a lot of hard work, a sacrifice of time, and stepping out of our comfort zone, but it leaves us feeling we have done something worthwhile with eternal value. It's not for nothing. It matters.

Are you currently involved in a difficult ministry situation or avoiding getting involved because you know it will be challenging?

If so, what makes it difficult? How is it taking a toll on you, or what scares you about getting involved?

How can others benefit from it?

What benefits are in it for you?

I encourage you to stay away from having a "duty mentality" in anything you are doing. Don't get involved in ministry out of guilt. Don't do it to try and earn God's favor. Don't substitute "doing things for God" in the place of having an authentic relationship with Him. If you are currently doing something, or you think you should, and this is your mentality, you should either stop doing it or change your mindset. Make it about you and God. Make it about what God wants to teach and show you.

Don't focus on the criticism you are receiving or the ways you have failed. Think about who is benefitting from your efforts. Focus on the fruit that is being produced—not only in the lives of others, but in your own heart. Bearing fruit isn't just about everyone else. It isn't about how many people you have brought into the kingdom or lives you have changed. It's about your own heart. What's in there? What's coming out? Are you producing the good fruit God says will be there when you walk by the Spirit, or are there a lot of rotten apples of bitterness, anger, conceit, envy, and strife hanging around?

The Fruit of the Spirit isn't something we can produce of ourselves. We cannot make up our minds to be more loving, joyful, peaceful, etc. and do it. The Fruit of the Spirit comes as it is defined: Of the Spirit. We must be abiding in Jesus, His truth, and His love for us. We must give ourselves over to Him and allow Him to take over our hearts. We must let Him transform us into a new creation.

What does Romans 12:2 say must be renewed in us?

It's about changing the way we think. It starts in the mind. It takes place when we know the truth and believe it. When we believe in His love for us. When we look at something we're doing and say, 'This isn't a lot of fun, but I know there's a purpose in it.' When we look at our own heart and can say, 'This is good.'

The enjoyment of God isn't just a feeling. It's a way of life. It's seen in the condition of the heart.

Based on this lesson and all the elements of joy, how would you rate your overall enjoyment of God? *(High, Medium High, Medium, Medium Low, or Low)*

Pray about how you can increase your enjoyment of Him.

More Water, More Fruit

On each side of the river stood the tree of life, bearing twelve crops of fruit, yielding its fruit every month.
Revelation 22:2

All of us are born with a desire to make a difference. Once we are old enough to realize the needs of others around us, we want to help. When our friend on the playground falls and scrapes her knee, we want to get her a Band-Aid to make her feel better. When our best friend gets dumped for the first time, we want to comfort her and assure her he was a jerk anyway. When we see someone going down a destructive path, we want to yell, "Stop! Don't do that!" And when someone we know is hurting, we want to do whatever we can to bring healing and peace and better days ahead.

The problem often isn't that we don't care. Sometimes it is. Sometimes we're so focused on our own problems and needs we can't see those who are hurting around us, let alone know how to help. But at other times, we're fully aware of a hurting heart, a broken relationship, family problems, and other needs, and we want to help, and we try to help, but our efforts don't really have the results we're hoping for.

Can you think of some needs others currently have? Think in terms of physical, emotional, and spiritual needs.

The Bible often talks about fruit. Fruit is something that is produced on trees and bushes and vines. Fruit is a source of nourishment and is usually rich in vitamins and other elements that are good for our physical bodies. And the same is true in terms of spiritual fruit. It is something that is produced, and it is something that is beneficial to us and those around us. Let's look at some places in the Bible that talk about how fruit is produced and what benefits it provides.

Genesis 1:11-12; 29
Fruit produced by:

Benefits:

John 15:1-11
Fruit produced by:

Benefits:

Revelation 22:2
Fruit produced by:

Benefits:

You don't have to be an expert in biology or a great Bible scholar to know plants bear fruit and plants need water to grow. This is a basic fact of life no one would argue. There are rules of nature that work a certain way, and we can't change them. We may want instantaneous fruit as soon as we plant a new seed in the ground, but it doesn't work that way.

Similarly, spiritual fruit isn't something that magically appears. There is a process involved. And God has told us the necessary steps. But too often we want to skip the process, toss in our own ingredients, and see the results we want; But it doesn't work.

Can you think of times you have tried to change your ways, or help someone else change theirs, using your own means rather than God's?

What were the results?

Read Galatians 5:22-23. What is the source of this kind of fruit?

Read John 7:37-39

Jesus talked about Living Water at different times and with different people. In this instance, He was speaking to a large crowd who had gathered for the Feast of the Tabernacle, an annual Jewish holiday that had been around for centuries. God had instructed Moses and the people living at that time to have an annual celebration to remind them of their time of living in the wilderness.

Read Deuteronomy 16:13-17

What attitude were the people to have at this Feast? (verse 14)

What promise was given? (verse 15)

What gift was to be brought by each man? (16-17)

Jesus was living during a turbulent time for the Jews. Their land was being overtaken by the Roman Government. The people were being oppressed spiritually by their own leaders. I don't know this for certain, but somehow I don't think there was a lot of joy taking place at the annual tradition. The people were going through the motions, but I don't think they were truly celebrating and remembering God's promise of blessing.

And in the middle of their annual feast, likely bathed in ritual and 'same ol', same ol', Jesus stands up and makes this great announcement: "If anyone is thirsty, come to me and drink." Were the people thirsty for something new? I bet they were. They were thirsty for hope and joy and love and peace. And Jesus says, "I'm it! I'm the source of what you need!"

Read Ezekiel 47:1-12

The Bible tells us that today, our bodies are the temple of the Holy Spirit (1 Corinthians 3:16; 6:19). And the vision Ezekiel had was of a future temple, not one that existed during his lifetime. It's talking about us. It's talking about a time when a literal temple (a man-made structure) would no longer be needed. God would no longer dwell in a structure built by human hands; He would dwell in us.

One of the key elements of this temple is the River flowing out of it. The water comes from the temple itself. And as Jesus tells us, He is the source of this life-giving water. But notice in Ezekiel 47, verses 3-6, there are different levels to this River. At first it is ankle-deep, then knee-deep and waist deep, and then finally it's too deep to touch the bottom. It's for swimming in! This can be a picture of how much of Jesus we are allowing to fill up our hearts. Is it only enough to get our feet wet? Or is it all-consuming, overtaking our hearts to the point we can't even touch the bottom?

The Fruit of the Spirit is dependent on how much of this water we're living in. When we take in a little of Jesus: a little of His love, a little of His truth, a little of His promises, the fruit comes accordingly. We have a little love to give to others, a little joy, a little peace, a little patience...

But when we're swimming in His love, His truth, His daily presence, His overflowing joy, His wonderful blessings...we're vessels of that to the same degree.

More water, more fruit. How much of the Living Water are you taking in? Drink deeply, sweet sister. It's yours for the taking. And the more YOU take in, the more of a difference you can make in the world around you.

The following is a poem I wrote as a prayer to God. Feel free to make it your prayer as well, or write your own, including what you need more of from Jesus.

More of You, Jesus
More of your grace
More of your love
More of your face

I need the water
That bears the fruit
To share Your love
That changes my heart

I need to believe
In all that You are
To trust in your promises
O Great Morning Star

For without Your Spirit
There is no hope
No joy and no life
To help others cope

But You are here
Your truth sets me free
So may I be
All that You are in me

The Right Solution

"I am the vine; you are the branches.
Those who remain in me, and I in them,
will produce much fruit.
For apart from me you can do nothing."
John 15:5 (NLT)

In the previous lesson we talked about bearing fruit. One of the characteristics of a healthy plant (that is, a healthy person who produces good fruit) is she takes in a good amount of the Living Water. Today's lesson is similar. Again it involves taking in a lot of Jesus, the difference that makes in our lives, and the difference it can make for others, but with a slightly different twist.

Just as we all want to make a difference, we also want to make good choices and live the right way. If we have a problem, we want to fix it. Or, if someone else has a problem, we want to provide them with the right solution. And for anything we face, there's probably an expert, a book, or some other form of wisdom we could look to for an answer: How to set goals and succeed; How to be a better friend; How to reach the lost with the Good News; How to get ready for college; How to...the list goes on and on.

And often reading a book on the subject or listening to the advice of others or going through counseling is helpful. Often the right solutions are there, and when we make the effort to take the necessary steps, we get the desired results. But not always. Sometimes what works for one person won't work for another. Sometimes two people can be in the exact same situation but need two different solutions. I've had people give me advice I can't use because it doesn't fit in with my personality or the personalities of others I'm dealing with. And sometimes we face things that are unpredictable or unprecedented. We would readily take the advice of someone who has been through the same thing, but there's no one to be found, or not the time to ask. What then? What do we do?

Think about your current circumstances. Is there anything you're facing where you really don't know what to do? Either because you haven't sought any guidance about it, or because you have, but nothing is working? Record what comes to mind.

Think also about others you may be trying to help, but the solution isn't clear.

Read the following and write any phrases that could apply to you or someone else in the circumstances you listed.

John 14:1-6

John 14:12-14

John 14:16-19

John 14:27

John 15:4-8

John 15:16-17

John 16:12-14

John 16:33

All of these words are spoken by Jesus to His closest disciples just before the time of His death. He knew they were going to be facing something they had never faced before. He knew they were going to be afraid, confused, and at a loss for what to do. And He leaves them with some final words that He hopes they will take to heart and remember as they face the unthinkable in the coming days.

And I believe He wants us to apply these same words to our lives today. Our trials may be very different than the ones His disciples faced, but the solution is the same.

One of the most difficult things I have faced in my life is raising an autistic child. I could listen to the advice of doctors, teachers, and other parents who had potential solutions, but they didn't always work. Just as each child is unique, each autistic child is unique. And there have been many times when the only voice I could rely on was the Voice of the Spirit.

The same is true for any of us when we face various complex situations. No two families are alike. No two friendships. No two losses. No two larger-than-life problems. And while we can listen to the wise advice of others at times, sometimes we can't. But we can *always* listen to the Spirit. Jesus always knows the right solution! And if we seek Him, we will find it.

Read John 16:12-14 again. What does Jesus say is the ultimate result of listening to the Spirit?

Have you found this to be true? Have you faced a situation where the end result was God being glorified through it?

Going back to what I was saying about my autistic son, I can certainly testify to the truth of Jesus' words. When I didn't know what to do, and I didn't have a lot of others who could guide me, Jesus was there whispering the right solutions in my ear, bringing the right people my way, and giving me the strength, peace, and joy to raise my son in the best possible way. And I take no credit for the very sweet, loving, well-adjusted, thriving boy that he is. I give all the credit to Jesus. And it's one of the greatest ways I can see His glory.

Refer to the phrases you recorded today from John 14-16. Write at least two of them on index cards to add to your collection.

Use the following prayer-prompts to talk to your Father about your current difficult circumstances or anything you need wisdom and direction for:

Father, I need...

Father, I'm hoping for...

Father, please help me to...

Father, I feel...

Father, I intercede today for...

Father, help me to love, forgive, teach, or help...

Created For Good

We are God's workmanship, created in Christ Jesus...
Ephesians 2:10

In the beginning of this devotional book, we looked at the meaning of repentance as "a change of thinking". Most of my spiritual growth in the last few years I can attribute to this. I read and I hear the same truths I've known for a long time, but I think of them in a different way. I discern the truth more clearly and realistically. Not just as truths to believe in my head, but to live out their implications in my life—and thus, to enjoy God more fully through a change of thought and action.

In John 10, Jesus calls Himself the Good Shepherd, and He likens us to sheep. He says, *"his sheep follow him because they know his voice. But they will never follow a stranger; in fact, they will run away from him because they do not recognize a stranger's voice."* And in John 8:43, He says, *"Why is my language not clear to you? Because you are unable to hear what I say."*

Listening to what God has to say isn't just about reading words from the Bible or listening to others teach what it says. Many people heard what Jesus had to say firsthand. They were standing right there listening to the words coming out of His mouth, but they didn't really "hear" Him. They didn't see how anything could be different than what they already had so set in their minds.

And I believe this is one of the greatest hindrances we have to enjoying God. We have it so fixed in our minds that He is demanding and condemning and to be greatly feared, we can't get past that. We have heard the words, *'It is by grace you have been saved,'* and yet we constantly stand ourselves against a measuring stick of trying to be good enough. And it kills our joy; It destroys our sweet fellowship with Him; It places a burden on us that is too heavy to carry.

Read John 10:1-10

According to these verses, what does Jesus want for us?

Do you feel you have ever been misled by a "stranger's" voice?

Have you ever been in church and felt the need to run away because of something that was being taught or something someone said to you? (whether or not you actually left)

There's a difference between *conviction* and *manipulative persuasion*. Often when we read the Bible or listen to Christian teaching, we will feel convicted of our sin. We will recognize ways we are not living in the truth and we will feel the need to confess our sin and change our behavior. This is good for us, and we should admit when we are wrong, ask God and others for forgiveness, and make every effort to go on our way and "sin no more" in this area of weakness. We may fail from time to time, but we recognize what we're doing isn't right and we're trying to overcome.

Manipulative persuasion, on the other hand, is leading people to believe something that isn't actually true. Partial truth may be there, but it's distorted or twisted. Often this will lead to feelings of guilt and may be disguised as conviction, but the difference is, it's not the Spirit's voice we are hearing. It's man's voice, or the voice of the enemy. Jesus calls these sources of manipulation, the 'thief', and their purpose is to steal, kill, and destroy. To steal your joy, to kill your faith, to destroy your sense of value and worth.

This kind of false teaching is not about cleaning up your heart and life to set you on the path to freedom. It's about putting a measuring stick in front of you and saying, 'You'll never be good enough.' It's about enslaving you into bondage (slavery) where you must earn God's favor and follow a set of rules or do certain things to attain worthiness. In Galatians 5:8, Paul says it this way: *This persuasion did not come from Him who calls you.*'(NASB)

Can you pinpoint some examples of how you have been subjected to this type of persuasion?

(This is one of the reasons reading the Bible on your own is so important. If you don't know the truth for yourself, it can be very difficult to know when you are being led down the wrong path.)

Read Ephesians 2:1-10

What wonderful truths are stated in verses 4-5?

Verse 6?

Did we earn any of this?

How is God glorified through us? (verse 7)

It's natural to feel we owe God something, and in reality we do. We owe Him much more than we can ever repay. But the beauty of God's grace is He doesn't want us to repay Him or even attempt to. When we do, it's no longer grace. His glory is best revealed in His great mercy and kindness to us, and anytime we try to earn His favor through good works or forced devotion, we are robbing Him of His glory.

Does this mean we just go on sinning so His glory can be seen all the more? No, because there's an even greater way His glory can be seen. Not only through forgiveness, but also through the benefits of choosing to live rightly today. Jesus wants us to admit and turn from our sin *so we can be rescued* from paths of self-destruction and pain. He not only forgives us of our sin, but He also has a better path for us. A path of goodness. A lifestyle of holiness we have the ability to live.

Ephesians 2:10 may be a familiar verse to you, but you may be hearing it wrong. I often hear the words of verses 8-9 spoken together to teach one truth, and then hear words of verse 10 taught by themselves to teach another truth, but they go together. And I think Paul explains the same concept a little more completely in Chapter Four.

Read Ephesians 4:17-24

What does Paul say in verses 22-24?

How is this related to God's grace?

We have been created for good. God didn't make a mistake when He made us. We are made in His image. We have His Heart! The same heart of mercy and grace and great kindness. And He wants us to walk in it. He wants us to live as we were created to live. Not to earn His favor, but because of His favor. How valuable are we to Him? Valuable enough to prepare a life of goodness for us. Not just to bring Him glory or benefit others, but also to benefit us. It's not about doing this good thing and that good thing, it's about the *good life* He wants us to have.

Choosing to do good works isn't a way to pay God back. It isn't a duty. It's a part of His kindness and great love for us. We are able to make the right choices. We are able to live a life of goodness. We are set up for a life of blessing. We are HIS workmanship. This is who He has graciously created us to be.

What are some things God has led you to lay aside? How has that been beneficial to you?

What qualities has God created in you?   How have they been beneficial to you?

What is God leading you to lay aside?   What benefits can you imagine as a result?

What qualities does God want to recreate or strengthen in you? What benefits can you imagine would be the result (for yourself and others)?

Joy Stealers

What has happened to all your joy?
Galatians 4:15

What robs us of joy? What takes away from our enjoyment of God? And what can bring it back when we have lost it? Today I am going to have you read selected verses from Paul's letters to the churches. He addressed several of these joy-stealers, and although these churches existed hundreds of years ago, I don't think their joy-stealers are too much different from ours today. Some of the exact issues might be different, but not the root of those issues. Keep in mind as you read specific verses that everything Paul says is usually a part of an overall theme he was addressing. Verses in Chapter Four of one letter, for example, can be related to words Paul spoke in Chapter One of that same letter. Paul has a tendency to interrupt himself and go off on "rabbit trails" to explain something that is important. But this can make it easy to forget what he was originally talking about! So, I'll try to guide you through the particular topics I want to emphasize on our topic of enjoying God.

Read Galatians 1:6-10

How would you describe Paul's mood here?

If he was speaking these words, what tone of voice would he have?

What was he so upset about?

What joy-stealer do you see in verse 10?

Trying to please people can be exhausting. While some may be pleased with what we say or do, others won't. We can't please everyone all of the time, and we can't even please just one person all of the time. And according to his own words, it's apparent Paul had stopped trying to be a people-pleaser. His agenda was to serve Christ and have His approval.

Do you think trying to win the approval of God can also be exhausting? Why?

Do you think Paul saw pleasing God as being a difficult thing to do?

Read Galatians 2:3-4 and 11-16

What was this "different gospel" Paul initially addressed in chapter one and then expounds on more here?

Is the "true gospel" Paul preached one of slavery or freedom? (2:4)

Do you always feel freed by the gospel of Christ or sometimes chained by it? How so?

In John 10:3, which direction does the Shepherd lead the sheep?

"Out" of slavery, not into it! (Am I sounding like Paul yet?)

Read Galatians 3:1-5

Write out the words Paul asks in verses 2-3.

How would you answer this for yourself?

Trying to earn the approval of God is a big-time joy-stealer! We can't do that! Number one, we will fail. Number two, it takes away from the grace of God. And number three, it robs us of the life we are meant to have in Christ.

Read Galatians 2:19-21

What is required in order to truly live for God? (verse 19)

What is the result of dying to the law? (verse 20)

What are we to live by? (verse 20)

What does Paul believe about the "Son of God"? (verse 20)

Do you believe that? How can believing in God's love for you help you to have more faith in Him rather than being focused on rules?

What question does Paul ask in Galatians 4:15?

The Galatians had lost sight of God's grace, and the consequence was an absence of joy. If you can relate to this, please hear me: God loves you no matter what. He wants you to live in that reality. He wants you to live in joy. If you feel you have lost your joy, go to Him and ask how you can get it back.

Abounding Love

And this is my prayer:
that your love may abound more and more...
Philippians 1:9

Today we are going to be looking at Paul's letter to the Philippians. It is quite different than the one he wrote to the Galatians, and it seems to me the church in Philippi was a pretty good church. It didn't have the problems of the Galatian church. In Philippians 1:7, Paul says this: 'All of you share in God's grace with me,' and there is no hint of Paul's mood being one of exasperation or an urgency to make radical changes. They weren't perfect, as we will see, but Paul's heart was very near to them and he greatly rejoiced in all that was right among them.

Read Philippians 1:3-11

What caused Paul to be thankful and pray with joy? (verses 4-5)

What encouraging words does he write in verse 6?

Do you need someone to speak these words over you today? Someone to say, *God has begun something wonderful in you and He won't stop! So take courage and hang in there because He has much to show you, teach you, and do through you.* If so, allow me to be that person. He will complete the work He has started in you!

Similarly, the words Paul writes in verses 7-8 are a good description of the way I feel about you. I have you in my heart. You are my dear sister, and I pray for you constantly. I hope it helps to know that. You are not alone in your journey of seeking God and learning to enjoy Him.

What was Paul's prayer for the Philippians? (verses 9-11)

What do you think love has to do with knowledge and understanding? Why are these elements necessary for love to abound?

Read Philippians 2:1-4

What benefits of knowing Christ does Paul mention? (verse 1)

What did Paul say would make his joy complete? (verse 2)

It appears the people understood the basic elements of living in the grace of God. They were united with Christ, living in His love, in fellowship with the Spirit, and had tender, compassionate hearts. And yet, they weren't really strong in the area of unity. They all believed the same things, but they weren't working together for a common purpose. They each had their own agenda and didn't see the big picture of what it meant to be a "church".

What characteristics does Paul list as possible weak points in their minds and hearts? (verse 3-4)

How could these attitudes steal their joy?

Which of these do you struggle with?

Unlike the letter to the Galatians where Paul was telling them they were heading completely in the wrong direction, his words to the people here are more in the spirit of, "You're doing great, but here's what you can do better." And it wasn't about them earning God's approval, it was about what was truly best for them as individuals and as a church. To be one in spirit and purpose. To have a common goal.

What was this goal according to Philippians 2:14-16?

What could block them from attaining this? (verse 14)

The words *grumbling, disputing, complaining,* and *arguing,* that your version may use, don't have the meaning of an open attitude of complaining or arguing like how you express your displeasure toward others, but rather the idea of an inward discontentment and doubt of what is right and true.

What we believe in our hearts will be exposed through our actions. If the "light of truth" is alive in your heart, you will shine like these verses talk about—like stars in the darkness, or bright lights in the world. But if your heart is full of doubt, discontentment, or other secret thoughts caused by a lack of belief or understanding of God and how much He loves you—you can't be a bright source of light for others. You must believe it for yourself first and live it—that's the most powerful testimony you can have.

What secret or unspoken doubts, complaints, or grumbling thoughts do you have toward God? Are you trying to teach or lead others in ways you don't fully embrace yourself?

Do you think any of these things could be a result of being taught things about God that aren't true—that you have been persuaded to believe rather than what the Bible clearly says? If so, you may want to do some self-study and allow God to speak the truth to you in these areas.

In Philippians 2:19, Paul mentions sending Timothy to them. Why do you think he knew that would be a good thing? (Hint: Timothy was a pastor.)

Churches need good leadership. If your church or youth group is weak in this area, ask God to bring those who are needed to help you and others be encouraged in your faith, go deeper into His love, and live by the Spirit. (Perhaps He is calling you to be a leader—pray about that too!)

Read Mark 12:28-31

Sometimes we can get so focused on loving God and doing things to bring others into His Kingdom, we walk all over those who are our brothers and sisters in Christ. This is not God's desire for us, or them. He wants us to "love more and more." Love is always the first rule. If we violate that one, we may as well not bother, no matter how noble our cause or how "right" we think we are. God is *always* more honored when we love than when we don't.

Is God asking you to love someone in your youth group, family, or elsewhere who is difficult to love? How could you apply the words from Philippians to this person?

Review this entire lesson. What do you hear Jesus saying to you today?

Rejoice!

Rejoice in the Lord always.
I will say it again: Rejoice!
Philippians 4:4

We have several "biggies" to challenge us today. By biggies I mean things that can really get in the way of our enjoyment of God, and we all struggle with them. Sometimes in huge proportions. Before you begin, pray for an open mind and heart that will allow God to speak to you in each of these challenging areas. Pray for a willingness to let go of things that may be greatly hindering your relationship with Jesus.

Read Philippians 3:1-11

What joy-stealer does Paul emphasize in verses 4-8?

What does putting confidence in our own greatness rob us of?

What did Paul consider to be greater than anything?

What do you think Paul means by being "found" in Christ? (v.9)

Knowing Christ is the goal. Knowing His love. Knowing His heart. Knowing what it's like to have unhindered fellowship with God. This is what we should focus on. Everything we do should have that end-result in mind, for ourselves and for others.

Read Philippians 4:4-7

What potential joy-stealer does Paul mention in verse 6?

What are you currently worried or anxious about?

Don't let these things steal your joy! Take time right now to pray about them and let Him give you peace. Write your prayer in your journal if you find that helpful.

What do you hear Him saying to you concerning these things?

Read verse 8. How can you see your worries in a positive light, or what else can you set your mind on?

Read Philippians 4:11-13

Joy-stealer? (Paul didn't have a problem with it, but we often do)

What is the secret to handling discontentment? (verse 13)

This verse is often taken out of context to mean we can do anything if we just have enough faith in the power of God to help us, and I believe that's true (Lord willing), but Paul is talking about overcoming a specific thing here: discontentment; which we honestly don't usually apply this truth to. We would rather move a mountain than learn to be content! The root of discontentment is believing we need this or that to be happy. But happiness doesn't come through things we have. Happiness comes through learning to be content in all circumstances.

But we can't do it on our own, only He can empower us to do that. And I believe the most effective way to receive His power is to believe we already have all we need in Him. His provision. His presence. And His love.

What things do you need to have contentment about?

Read Philippians 4:4. How can learning to rejoice in the Lord make a difference in your current thinking about these things?

Review the answers you gave in this lesson. What stands out to you most?

What verses would be good to memorize? Write them on index cards and work on committing them to memory.

Free To Serve

You were called to be free.
Galatians 5:13

The Christian life is often lived out in paradoxes. A paradox is a statement or set of truths that seem contradictory, but they're not. Jesus sometimes spoke this way. We are going to be looking at a few such times, along with Paul's writings that also contain paradoxes. Our focus is the freedom we have as children of God, and yet freedom does not always mean we can do whatever we want. Similarly, those who live sinful lives often think of themselves as living in freedom, but in reality they're slaves to sin. See what I mean by a paradox?

When we talk about enjoying God, there are often paradoxes involved. We may see a particular command as being restrictive, when in reality it leads to freedom. We may be resistant to Christ's leading because we don't want to submit and surrender things to Him, and yet when we do, that's where the joy is. To see the truth in paradoxes, we must learn to think differently. We must learn to see God *always* has our best interests in mind, and often we need Him to rescue us from our wrong thinking and desires.

What paradoxes do you see in Christ's words in the following? (Consider how lowly servants would normally be treated.)

John 12:26

John 15:14-15

Read Galatians 5:1. Why did Christ set us free?

Read Galatians 5:13-21

What should our freedom in Christ <u>not</u> be used for? (verse 13)

What are some examples of this? (15, 19-21)

How could these take away from our freedom?

What should our freedom be used for? (verses 13-14)

Who comes to mind when you think of 'serving others in love'?

This is a paradox I want to emphasize. When we know we are free, when we realize how much we are loved by God, it sets us free to love others more freely. We are not in bondage to needing their love in return because God's love for us is enough. Someone else may need our love until they can learn to see how loved by God they are. He calls us to be an expression of His love without needing anything from them.

And serving someone in love, as strange as it sounds, actually leads us into greater freedom. Our hearts are set free from needing everyone to cooperate with us or give us something in return for our efforts. If they do, great. But if they don't, no biggie. We're still loved and valued by God just as much as ever. And if we have any needs others don't meet for us, He will.

Read Galatians 5:22-26

Serving others requires the elements of the Fruit of the Spirit. We need love, joy, peace, patience, kindness, goodness, faithfulness, gentleness, and self-control. And Jesus promises to give us these when we walk by His Spirit.

What does Jesus say in John 14:26 about His Spirit?

In order to walk in the Spirit, we must listen to Him through our hearts and through the words Jesus spoke, which we have written for us in the Gospels (Matthew, Mark, Luke & John). Remember Him saying His words are spirit and life? I can personally testify that they are, and taking to heart the words of Christ and living them out in our lives is the key to a Spirit-led life.

How are you doing on your Bible reading and journaling? I hope you have been doing that along with the devotions in this book, and if you have, I'm sure you've found that valuable. As you can see, there aren't a lot of lessons left, and I have purposely kept my devotional books to a minimum.

I could write many more, I'm sure, and another one may be coming after this one, but I really don't want you to be relying on me and my insight. You can listen to Jesus just the same as me. And it's not only about knowing the truth and understanding it, but it's also about knowing the Teacher. And I can't do that for you. That's up to you. You are His sheep, and you can hear His voice.

What do *you* hear Jesus saying to you today?

Valued Servants

"I no longer call you servants."
John 15:15

What does it take to be a servant of God? A follower of Jesus? A disciple? When Jesus calls us to follow Him, He is looking for something specific in us. To teach us something. But I think a lot of us have the wrong idea about what it is.

The particular parable Jesus taught we are going to be looking at today is one Jesus speaks specifically to His disciples, to those who were committed to following Him; and He tells it at the end of a very long dialogue where He is trying to explain to some religious leaders what His Kingdom is really about. He tells several parables concerning "the lost" and His desire for them to come to Him. He also talks about money, faith, and truly knowing God.

Read Luke 17:1-10

Who do you think Jesus is referring to in verses 1-2? (Hint: Whom was Jesus talking to in Chapter 16? See vs. 14-15)

What does Jesus say in 17:3-4?

Jesus is teaching them about a new law: the law of mercy and grace. In His words to 'rebuke' those who sin, the word rebuke has the idea of a loving kind of correction. To speak the truth in love, not harshness. To correct the sin without devaluing the sinner. And He also speaks of unlimited forgiveness toward those who have wronged them.

Obviously the disciples find this concept difficult and cry out, "Increase our faith!" But Jesus responds by saying, *"If you have faith as a mustard seed, you can say to this mulberry tree, 'Be pulled up by the roots and be planted in the sea,' and it would obey you."* (NKJV)

Some translations of this verse say, *"If you have faith as small as a mustard seed..."* But I don't believe this is accurate because while a mustard seed is small, the faith of a mustard seed is not a small amount of faith. It takes a lot of faith to become so much more than how you start out, as the mustard seed does by becoming the largest of all garden plants. And that's what the disciples needed to do. They needed to become so much more than they were, and Jesus is saying, 'If you can believe in who I have created you to be, you can do it!'

What are some areas of weakness you need to have the faith of a mustard seed to overcome?

Do you believe you can be more loving, forgiving, and merciful because of who you are in Christ? With whom could you apply this truth?

I need to be more loving, forgiving, and patient with...

What parable does Jesus tell in verses 7-10?

Do you think He wanted them to view themselves this way? (Read John 15:14-16 for the answer.)

I believe some translations tell this parable in Luke 17 incorrectly. In verse 10, the word *should* is added. It is not a part of the original Greek, and it changes the meaning of what Jesus is saying. I believe He's saying, 'This is how you see yourselves: You think of yourselves the way you would think of a slave. You would expect dutiful service from him. You would expect him to put your needs above his own. And you wouldn't bother thanking him for his service because that's his job. You would see him as a slave and nothing more.'

But is that the view Jesus wanted them to have? Is that the view He wants us to have of ourselves? I don't think so. The way people view servants and the way God views His servants is vastly different. We cannot put our own ways and tendencies on God. He is not like us. His ways are higher than our ways. His view of us is different than we often think. If you go back to Chapter Fifteen of Luke, you will read about the parable of the man who had two sons. One son squandered his father's money until he had to come back to beg for his father's forgiveness, and the other son remained. But neither one of them really understood how much his father loved him. The lost son didn't think his father would welcome him as anything but a hired hand, and the dutiful son is upset when his father throws a big party for his wayward brother.

What does the "dutiful" son say in Luke 15:29?

How does the Father respond?

Serving Jesus isn't about duty. It isn't about doing things and living a certain way just because we're told to do so. It isn't about serving Him and everyone else while we go without having our own needs met.

It's about being with Him. It's about receiving the blessings He has for us so we have something to give. It's about believing we are loved and valued and being much more with Him than we could ever be on our own.

To live the law of mercy and grace is what it takes to be a servant of God. But to live it, we must first receive it. And we don't receive it by thinking of ourselves as dutiful slaves, but as beloved children.

In what ways do you see yourself as a beloved child of God?

This is a poem I wrote as a personal testimony of the way Jesus has taught me to view myself in His eyes. I hope you are blessed by it and believe in its truth for yourself.

Back To Love

When I was young
I believed in Your love
I had nothing to offer You
I just knew I was Yours

You gave me a heart
To love You in return
To love others as You loved me
And I was happy

When I grew older, others said
You must give Him more
It's not enough to just believe
You must prove your love

I became dutiful
Loyal committed and sacrificial
I was good and deserving
I was better than most

So why did I feel so bad
Why was I always sad
Where was the joy
Where was the peace

It's in My love for you, You said
You're not My slave
You're My child
Be still

I stopped running ahead
I waited
You picked me up
You carried me

Back to Love
Back to Joy
Back to Peace
Back to the Truth

And it's sweet
And it's good
And it's me
And it's You

It's the way
You always
Want it
To be

It's the way
I always
Know it
Can be

The Open Gate

Jesus said, "I tell you the truth,
I am the gate for the sheep."
John 10:7

Imagine this scene: Small town life, a friendly neighborhood, the hum of a lawnmower going a few houses away, a dog barks, a car drives leisurely down the street. You're ten years old, walking home from school. Your house is just up the street, and you can already taste that chocolate chip cookie your mom has waiting for you. You hurry along a little faster. When you arrive, the front gate of the white picket fence is open, and you walk right through it. Up the path and up the front steps and then you step inside. The familiar things are there to greet you. The smells of home, the sound of the dryer going in the laundry room, the sight of your mom standing in the kitchen, waiting to greet you and serve the milk and cookies your mouth is watering for. Nothing out of the ordinary. Just what you expect. The peace and joy and love of home.

Read John 10:1-10

In this word-picture scenario Jesus describes, what does Jesus call Himself?

Read John 10:14-15

What does Jesus call Himself in these verses?

Why do you think Jesus is both the gate and the shepherd?

Read Revelation 4:1-3

Is the door to Heaven open or closed?

What is the first thing John sees in Heaven?

Who do you think is sitting there?

When Jesus calls Himself the gate for the sheep, He's talking about a gate that is open. He is not the gatekeeper who opens and closes the door, but rather He is the door that is always open. He is the access point to the life of abundance, safety, and freedom He describes.

He is also the shepherd. He is the one who will care for us, meet our needs, and lead us in a life worth living. He will never take anything from us, but only give. In the scene with the ten-year-old coming home from school, there was never any doubt that the house, the open gate, and the cookie would be there. When something good is familiar and predictable, there is a sense of peace and joyful expectancy.

Read John 10:14-15 again. What does Jesus say He will do for the sheep?

How is this related to His love for us?

How does He compare our relationship with Him to His relationship with His Father?

The key to this entire passage is the love the Shepherd has for the sheep. The gate is open. He wants us to come to Him. He wants to lead us. He has good things waiting. And the only thing we have to do is walk through the gate—to believe in His love. He knows us, and He wants us to know Him. Closely. Intimately. Familiar. Predictable. Like a Son knows His Father and a Father knows His Son. This is His Kingdom. This is what it's all about. Trusting Him. Knowing Him. Living in Him.

Read Psalm 37:3-7

When we delight in God, when we believe He is enjoyable, when we trust Him; we know what's coming. We know He will be faithful. We know we are safe. We know there is abundance and peace and goodness awaiting us. Maybe our current circumstances are dark, maybe we don't know exactly when the light is coming or how things will work out, but we know it's coming. The right solution. The better days. The unpredictable surprise He has waiting for us. And yet it's not a surprise, because we knew He would do something amazing all along.

Enjoy safe pasture, dear one. Jesus has promised you that. In His love there is always something to delight in. Are you living loved today?

What God Enjoys

The Lord delights in those who fear him,
who put their hope in his unfailing love.
Psalm 147:11

When I think about enjoying someone, I tend to focus primarily on what I enjoy about them. What I like, how I enjoy them, what they give me that makes them so enjoyable. But I often don't think of the other side of it: what they enjoy about me. I do this with my husband, my children, my family members, and close friends; and I also do this with God.

But when we're involved in a relationship with someone, it's important to remember that just as there are things we enjoy about them, there are things they enjoy about us. This is what makes a relationship more fulfilling and complete—when there is enjoyment on both sides. So today we're going to look at what God enjoys about you.

Read the following verses and record what brings God pleasure or delight, what pleases Him, or what is His desire.

Psalm 147:11

Proverbs 11:20

Proverbs 12:22

Proverbs 15:8

Jeremiah 9:23-24

Luke 12:29-32

Ephesians 1:7-10

Psalm 149:1-5

I love Psalm 149 that shows the mutual delight of God and His people. And I don't think it can be any other way. We delight in God, and He delights in us. When we are enjoying Him, He will be enjoying us because we will be living according to His love and truth, and that's what He wants.

I cannot tell you how sick I became a few years ago of a popular Christian phrase that said, 'It's not about us.' Have you heard people say that? I know when people do, they think they're honoring God, but they're not. It has to be about us, or it's meaningless. God's love for us is meaningless. God's truth is meaningless. We're meaningless!

But we're not. We are so valuable to Him. He gave His life for us. He shares the truth with us so we can have an abundant life. He loves us because He can't not love us. God is love, and we are the primary object of that love!

God delights in us. Just think of it! Don't try to understand why. Don't think you can earn it. Just believe. Just live it.

Write the phrase, IT IS ABOUT ME, five times.

Read Psalm 149:2-5 again and write out the words. Underline the words (or any words related to) joy, gladness, and delight.

How can you rejoice in your Maker?

In what ways does God rejoice in you?

Amazing Joy

We were eyewitnesses of His majesty.
2 Peter 1:16

As we near the end of our journey together, I want to direct your attention once again to a moment when Jesus' disciples were caught up in the enjoyment of God. They probably didn't realize it at the time, like we often miss moments Jesus is trying to engage with us in a memorable, life-changing way. But they still experienced the glory, and I'm sure it had a profound impact on the way they followed Jesus during the three years He was with them, and in the many years that followed when He was still with them, but in a different way: the same way we have Jesus with us today through the presence of His Spirit.

Read Luke 5:1-11

What does Jesus do in verse 3?

What does Jesus tell Simon (Peter) to do in verse 4?

Why did Peter obey? (verse 5)

What happened? (6-7)

How does Peter respond to this? (8-10)

What was the end result of the "big catch"?

Following Jesus doesn't begin with following Jesus. It begins with Jesus giving us an opportunity to observe His majesty. This wasn't the first time Peter had encountered Jesus, but it was the moment that caused him to follow Him wholeheartedly. And I love how it begins: Jesus got into Peter's boat.

For Peter, his boat was his life. Fishing was something he loved, something he was good at, and something necessary for his survival. It was his work, his passion, his present, and his future. Notice that Peter wasn't one of the men in the crowd who was eager to hear Jesus speak. He was working. He was busy. He was tired after a long night of bad fishing. And this is where Jesus meets him.

Can you think of a time when Jesus has met you in this way?

Look at verse 5 again. How eager do you think Peter was to do as Jesus said?

Personally, I don't think Peter was as agreeable to Jesus' idea as the text may imply. He may have been a little short with Jesus, even sarcastic: 'We've been working all night! But if Yooouuu say so.' (Who does this guy think he is?) But Jesus was in the boat, and Peter did what He said, and Jesus showed him something miraculous in those deep waters. And, to put it mildly, Peter is impressed. Awestruck with wonder, you might say. (Jesus scared him out of his mind!)

What "boat" are you currently in? School, friendships, sports, work, family-life, challenges? Are you currently facing some deep waters?

Have you let Jesus into your boat? If so, in what ways?

How do you think you could let Him be more involved?

I encourage you to let Jesus awe you with His presence and power, just as He did with Peter. Let Him show you something amazing. Let Him show you what only He can do.

What does 2 Peter 1:16 say?

Can you say the same thing? How have you seen Him?

How could your current circumstances (good or bad) be an opportunity for you to enjoy God?

In Spirit and In Truth

The joy of the LORD is your strength.
Nehemiah 8:10

In my research and study of putting this devotional book together, I came across an interesting historical event for the people of Israel I would like to leave you with on the subject of enjoying God. When I first began writing this devotional, I wasn't entirely certain what I had to say was valid, or that I could express it to others with the weight of Scripture behind me. I knew I was experiencing it, but because I had been taught so little on the subject of enjoying God, I couldn't help but wonder: Is it really in there?

Through this study I hope you have found that it is, and I know my own belief and experience of enjoying God has increased, so I thank all of you who kept asking me when my next devotional book was coming out. Believing something about God and experiencing it in my own life is one thing; but to be taught something by His spoken word to me personally, and then to see those same words spoken to His people in the past is more exciting than I can put into words. I guess you could say in writing a devotional book about enjoying God, I have only learned to enjoy Him all the more.

Before you read this first passage, let me give you a little background on the time this scene takes place. Nehemiah had been instructed by God to rebuild the wall surrounding Jerusalem. The people who had returned from exile in Babylon were living in ruins, and Nehemiah organizes everyone together and brings many of the supplies needed to reconstruct the wall. After a lot of hard labor and some opposition to their effort, the wall is completed and the people are able to live in peace once again. This is where we pick up the story.

Read Nehemiah 8:1-12

What book did Ezra read from?

Were the people eager to listen?

Who was listening? (verse 3)

What does it say in verse 6?

What role did the Levites play in the reading of the Book of the Law? (verses 7-8)

What were the people doing while it was being read and explained to them? (verse 9)

What did Nehemiah instruct them to do instead? (9-10)

Why were they to have such joy? (verses 10, 12)

There are several different words in the Old Testament that are translated as the word *joy*. The one most used has the idea of cheerfulness or lightheartedness: a carefree disposition that is expressed in obvious ways. Another word for joy, and the one found in Nehemiah 8:10 means *rejoicing*, and it can be an action or a feeling of someone who is glad, happy, or delighted. Rejoicing implies that you are full of joy.

So, according to Nehemiah (and God, I assume, since Nehemiah was following Him), rejoicing and being full of joy is the secret to remaining strong. The word *strength* as it is used here has the idea of a secure place. What I think Nehemiah is saying to these people who had been living in a very insecure state after their wall had been broken down is this: 'Rejoicing in the LORD will keep you safe. It's not about the wall of the city, it's about your heart. It's about your faith in Him. It's about your enjoyment of Him.'

Read Psalm 100

How are we to worship God? (verses 1-2, 4)

What are we to believe? Why should we worship in this way? (verses 3 & 5)

Because we are His! Because we have listened and followed His voice. Because He is good and faithful and He loves us! Is this why you worship God? Is this why you are following Him? Do you really believe the words you sing to Him? Do you truly believe He is worthy of your praise?

Read John 4:19-24

Remember the woman at the well? Remember the woman Jesus offered Living Water to? Remember how He wanted to fill her emptiness? This is the same woman Jesus speaks these words to. How does He say we must worship Him?

It's not about the place or the means. It's about the heart. And if we are going to rejoice in all that God is, and all He has done for us, we must believe it, and we must live it. We must enjoy Him! This is not an option. This is the kind of worshipers the Father seeks. He's looking for it!

Why do you think He wants us to worship Him in spirit and in truth?

How do you think this is related to enjoying Him?

I hope you do enjoy Him. If not yet, that you will. And if you feel like you're just getting started, know that it is a journey. These people of Jerusalem had been through a lot. They certainly had many reasons to not have much joy in their hearts. But God was faithful to them, and they saw that. And when they were ready to change their ways and live according to God's ways, He renewed their minds so they could. He changed their thinking. He made them see it was about joy, not duty. It was about them and the good plans He had for them.

I love the beginning of Nehemiah 8:10 where it says, *"Go and enjoy choice food and sweet drinks, and send some to those who have nothing prepared."* Do you see it? He wanted them to enjoy Him first, to taste and see His goodness, and then they could pass on the joy to others. May we be a generation of Jesus Followers who do the same.

What do you hear Jesus saying to you today?

Journaling Format

Date_____
Today I read_____

What does it say?

What does this mean in my own words?

How can this specifically apply to my life?

What changes do I need to make because of what it says?

How can this be an encouragement to me?

What do I hear God saying to me?

What is my response to Him?

Prayer Guide

Father, I need...

Father, I'm hoping for...

Father, please help me to...

Father, I feel...

Father, I intercede today for...

Father, help me to love, forgive, teach, or help...

*I'd love to hear how God has used
this devotional-study to touch your heart.*

Write me at:

living_loved@yahoo.com

Printed in Great Britain
by Amazon

73202327R00092